STEAM RAILWAYS

FINAL OPERATIONS IN THE SOUTHERN REGION AND THE EARLY PRESERVATION YEARS

DAVID REED

AMBERLEY

For my late parents, Margaret and Jimmy Reed,
who fostered my enthusiasm for trains
and encouraged my interest in photography.

First published 2021

Amberley Publishing
The Hill, Stroud
Gloucestershire, GL5 4EP

www.amberley-books.com

Copyright © David Reed, 2021

The right of David Reed to be identified as
the Author of this work has been asserted in
accordance with the Copyrights, Designs and
Patents Act 1988.

ISBN 978 1 3981 1013 7 (print)
ISBN 978 1 3981 1014 4 (ebook)

British Library Cataloguing in Publication Data.
A catalogue record for this book is available from
the British Library.

Origination by Amberley Publishing.
Printed in the UK.

Introduction

In 1967, the year that steam trains finished on the Southern Region of British Railways, I was a teenager studying for my GCE 'O' level exams. Through school friends I became aware that the steam locomotives that we had taken for granted were due to be withdrawn on Sunday 9 July of that year and I determined to make my own record of Southern steam's final operations.

There was no sophisticated 35 mm camera or lineside permit for me, and I am afraid there may be some less than pin-sharp images in this collection. For the photographers among you, I borrowed my mother's 'Purma Plus' camera, which is still in my possession. It was made in the early 1950s so is nearly as old as me. It had a fixed focus f6.3 lens and three shutter speeds of 1/25th, 1/150th and 1/500th second. I used Kodak Ektachrome-X colour slide film, which had a film speed of 64 ASA, and despite the best efforts of a Phillips Exposure Calculator, I quickly learned that I was limited to the two slower shutter speeds.

The 127 roll film gave me sixteen photographs per film, each square in format and slightly larger than a 35 mm transparency. I took the films to a local chemist to be processed, the cost of this and the film purchase being quite a lot more expensive than 35 mm film. In those far-off days my pocket money had to be juggled between photography, buying model railway equipment, purchasing railway magazines and saving to go on a British India educational cruise on the SS *Nevasa*.

As a family we lived in Basingstoke, not far from the South Western main line from Waterloo. My early trainspotting days were spent with my brother, Roger, by the lineside at Winklebury, between Basingstoke station and Worting Junction, a pleasant walk across the fields behind our home.

However, by early 1967 I had discovered Basingstoke locomotive shed and this picture of me at fifteen years of age, with my younger brother Roger, was taken by my father at Basingstoke shed on 2 July 1967, the week before steam finished.

By this time the Waterloo to Exeter services were being hauled by Western Region Warship Class diesel-hydraulic locomotives but the Bournemouth, Weymouth and some local Salisbury services were still in the hands of the Merchant Navy, West Country, Battle of Britain and BR Standard steam locos. By dint of careful pocket money management I was able to take a trip to Bournemouth and Poole to photograph the last Southern steam train operations. The results are portrayed in this book, a schoolboy's very personal memories of a significant period in his life.

In 1967 the Waterloo–Bournemouth and Weymouth line had become the last true steam-operated main line in England. Although there were pockets of steam operation in north-west England, which lasted into 1968, if you wanted to experience high speed main line steam traction at its best the Bournemouth line was the place to be. The locomotives were generally looking rather run down and by this time most had lost their nameplates and cast smokebox numberplates. However, the engine crews were obviously keen and made the most of the fairly straight and relatively easily graded London & South Western Railway main line. I was lucky to experience a couple of good runs between Basingstoke, Southampton and Bournemouth, which led to me taking my final operations pictures, which follow.

One particular run on the Up Channel Islands Boat Train on 26 May was very exciting. I was standing in the front vestibule of the first coach and there were two long wheelbase vans immediately behind the loco. As we sped between Winchester and Basingstoke I remember the two vans were bouncing about in a most alarming manner. And this was on an uphill section of line!

When main line steam finished we had to search out preserved steam locomotives. In the late 1960s there was nothing comparable with the heritage lines we are used to today, and there were only a few preserved locomotives bought directly out of BR service. The days of mass preservation of locos from Dai Woodham's Barry scrapyard were far in the future, let alone the repatriation of engines from abroad and the creation of new-build locomotives like *Tornado*.

I was fortunate that the Longmoor Military Railway was reasonably close and my father took little persuading to take us to visit railway open days there. Bulleid Pacifics *Blackmore Vale*

and *Clan Line*, together with David Shepherd's 9F 2-10-0 *Black Prince* and Class 4MT 4-6-0 *The Green Knight*, were based there with some other locos until the system closed. Journeys to family holidays spent in the West Country almost always involved a tea break at Buckfastleigh station, where the previous picture was taken in the company of GWR pannier tank No. 1369.

On completion of my GCE 'A' level exams in 1970 I was very fortunate to join British Rail Southern Region's Railway Studentship Training Scheme. This was one of many schemes run by BR for school leavers and graduates in a variety of railway operating, commercial and engineering disciplines. I was lucky indeed to be able to work for an industry in which I had so much interest. One of my first actions on starting to earn a regular salary was to treat myself to a 35 mm single lens reflex camera. It was only a Russian Zenith but the cost of photography was significantly reduced and the flexibility was greatly increased. Some of the later pictures in this book were taken with this camera.

I have included three or four photographs taken by my late father, including the two featured in this introduction. My father fostered my interest in railways from a very early age and my mother encouraged my teenage photographic endeavours by allowing me to use her Purma camera. I owe grateful thanks to them both.

My thanks are also due to John Dawson, a friend and work colleague of many years. John has seen the original colour slides on several occasions and he encouraged me to have them published. I didn't make detailed notes at the time many of the photographs were taken, so I trust my recollection back to my schooldays has not led to too many errors. John has added some useful information and corrections to my text. I also thank my wife, Margaret, for her support during the preparation of this book and for checking my manuscript.

Thanks are also due to the many businesses, organisations and individuals that have contributed to the success of the railway preservation movement, and I trust this collection of photographs will do justice to their early days. Some venues no longer exist and others have gone on to become the well-known heritage railway attractions, which provide so much enjoyment for volunteers and visitors alike, as well as employment in traditional engineering and other fields.

Apart from the three or four pictures taken by my father, all the photographs in this publication are my own work and none have been published previously. Photography generally and of trains in particular has given me tremendous enjoyment over the years. I count myself immensely lucky that, although young at the time, I was able to experience and record the final operations of the last steam-powered main line in Britain.

I hope you will enjoy my photographic record of steam's final operations and the early preservation years.

Final Operations in the Southern Region

On shed at Basingstoke on a sunny 29 January 1967 we see West Country Class No. 34025 *Whimple*, Standard 2-6-4T No. 80139 and West Country Class No. 34047 *Callington*.

One of the last of the class of 155 locomotives, Standard Class 4 2-6-4 tank loco No. 80152 takes a breather at Basingstoke on 29 January 1967.

Bulleid Pacific No. 34047 *Callington*, complete with nameplates and 'West Country Class' scrolls, catches the late afternoon sun while being turned at Basingstoke shed on 29 January 1967.

West Country Class No. 34025 *Whimple* heads out of Basingstoke towards Waterloo on 4 April 1967.

Behind a cloud of smoke No. 34104 *Bere Alston* shunts off the Reading line at the west end of Basingstoke on 4 April 1967. In the background some firemen are attending to an Esso fuel tanker, en route either to or from Fawley oil refinery, which has been liberally smothered in foam, maybe due to a hot axle box. In those far-off days staff could walk across a high-speed main line without a high visibility vest.

Battle of Britain Class No. 34056 *Croydon* leaves Basingstoke heading an express for Waterloo on 4 April 1967. She still has in place the sturdy 'Meccano bracket' to which the nameplate and Royal Air Force crest would have been bolted. After serving as our main airport from the 1920s, Croydon aerodrome became a fighter station in the Battle of Britain and from 1943 was used by RAF Transport Command to take troops to and from Europe.

Immediately recognisable from her extended smoke deflectors is West Country Class No. 34006 *Bude*, seen on shed at Basingstoke on 4 April 1967. The deflectors were extended to improve smoke clearance prior to the Locomotive Exchanges in 1948 and never reverted to the standard size.

Merchant Navy Class No. 35008 *Orient Line*, still complete with her nameplates but minus her smokebox numberplate, waits to take the empty stock of a westbound local service into Basingstoke station in the early evening of 5 April 1967. Note the electric indicator light on the right side of the smokebox door just below the white headcode disc.

Moments later as *Orient Line* draws forward, West Country Class No. 34037 *Clovelly* speeds past with the Up 'Bournemouth Belle' Pullman train. At this time of evening my camera's fixed lens aperture and 1/25th second shutter speed can hardly cope with all the action!

Coming fast out of a bright evening sun east of Basingstoke is No. 34044 *Woolacombe* on the Up 'Bournemouth Belle'. Taken on 8 April 1967, this picture shows the maroon Mark 1 full brake leading the train of umber and cream Pullman coaches.

Merchant Navy Class No. 35013 *Blue Funnel*, complete with name, number plates and express train headcode, is gently simmering in the shed yard at Basingstoke on 8 April 1967. The Merchant Navy locos were named after shipping lines that used the Southern Railway docks at Southampton. In her unrebuilt form, No. 35013 was named at Waterloo station on 17 April 1945.

BR Standard Class 4MT 4-6-0 No. 75077, with double chimney, waits with a van in the Down side sidings opposite the new panel signal box at Basingstoke on 8 April 1967. The class was designed at Brighton Works and she was built at Swindon in 1955. She carries a very colourful smokebox numberplate, which tends to emphasise the soot and dirt elsewhere.

West Country Class No. 34025 *Whimple* takes the Reading branch from Basingstoke on 9 April 1967 with the 'Hampshire Branch Lines Rail Tour'. The tour ran from Waterloo via Salisbury, Southampton, the Fawley and Lymington Pier branches, Basingstoke, Reading, Ascot, Aldershot, Guildford, Staines and back to Waterloo. Ten locos were involved and *Whimple* hauled the excursion between Brockenhurst and Ascot via Basingstoke and Reading.

Standard Class 4MT 2-6-0 No. 76066 has evidently filled up with coal and shunts past the turntable at Basingstoke shed on 15 April 1967. She was built at Doncaster works in 1956 and was one of the class fitted with a large tender with increased water capacity.

With her cylinder cocks open, West Country Class No. 34102 *Lapford* shunts past the turntable at Basingstoke locoshed on 28 April 1967. *Lapford* and No. 34023 *Blackmore Vale* were the last two unrebuilt Bulleid Pacifics left in service at the very end of steam. *Lapford* was built in 1950 at Eastleigh works and has the 9-feet-wide cab of the later locos.

A very grubby No. 34025 *Whimple* arrives at Basingstoke headed for Bournemouth on 26 May 1967. *Whimple* headed our outward service on the occasion of a trip with some school friends to Southampton, Bournemouth and Poole to see and photograph Southern Steam, as recorded in the following sequence of pictures.

The loco was built in 1946 and numbered in the Bulleid system as No. 21C125. She was rebuilt at Eastleigh in 1957 when the air-smoothed casing was removed, having covered half a million miles. Originally named *Rough Tor*, she was renamed *Whimple* in 1948. On withdrawal in 1967 she had covered nearly 873,000 miles. This loco seemed to follow me about in 1967 and several of my pictures are of *Whimple*.

Note the Western Region Diesel Mechanical Multiple Unit in the bay platform behind. These trains did not carry unit numbers and the enthusiastic spotters used to note down the individual carriage numbers.

Photographed from our train to the west, No. 34037 *Clovelly* was built in 1946. She waits at Bevois Park sidings with an Up train of parcels stock ready to head east towards Basingstoke, joining the main line just west of St Denys station on 26 May 1967.

Seen in a classic view under the signal gantry, No. 34025 *Whimple* awaits departure west from Southampton Central station on 26 May 1967. Notice the welded patch on the lower edge of the tender and hearty dent at the rear. Several Bulleid Pacific tenders had to be rebodied over the years due to wear and tear.

Merchant Navy Class No. 35028 *Clan Line* on shed at Bournemouth with Crompton diesels (later Class 33) and another Bulleid Pacific in the shadows on 26 May 1967. The blue Crompton represents the exciting new future, having been modified with waist-height jumper cables and repainted in blue and yellow for push-pull working with 4TC trailer units between Bournemouth and Weymouth. The term Crompton was derived from their Crompton-Parkinson electrical equipment.

Standard Class 4MT 2-6-4T No. 80011 at Bournemouth, also on 26 May 1967, grubby and minus her smokebox numberplate. The Down platform at Bournemouth Central was very long, being able to accommodate two trains, and gave a wonderful view of the locomotive shed and locos in the shed yard.

West Country Class No. 34036 *Westward Ho* was built at Brighton Works in 1946 and rebuilt at Eastleigh in 1960, and simmers on shed at Bournemouth on 26 May 1967.

Standard Class 4MT 2-6-0 No. 76005, rather grubby and minus her smokebox numberplate, poses in the cavernous interior of Bournemouth Central station on 26 May 1967. Notice the Post Office trolley on the left. In the 1960s large quantities of mail and parcels were conveyed in the brake vans of passenger trains and station dwell times had to allow for loading and unloading to take place.

Ivatt Class 2 2-6-2T No. 41224 is shed pilot at Bournemouth on 26 May 1967. She was built at Crewe in the year of railway nationalisation – 1948. Note the elevated signal box above the Down platform canopy and the blue 4TC set, complete with orange curtains, in the station platform.

Very clean and presentable, even if minus her nameplates, West Country Class No. 34023 *Blackmore Vale* shunts in Bournemouth shed yard on 26 May 1967. Attached to the concrete fence above the rear of the tender can just be glimpsed the sign 'Quiet Please – Residential Area' encouraging enginemen to keep their locos quiet. Preservation beckoned for No. 34023 a few months later.

Seen from the footbridge, Ivatt Class 2 2-6-2T No. 41320 rushes light engine across the level crossing at Poole station on 26 May 1967.

In this view No. 41320 is seen later that day banking the Channel Islands Boat Train up Parkstone bank. Poole Harbour is visible in the background.

Merchant Navy Class No. 35008 *Orient Line* is depicted leaving Southampton Central station and heading towards the tunnel under the Civic Centre, also on 26 May 1967.

Battle of Britain Class No. 34087 *145 Squadron* is ready to head west from Basingstoke on 30 May 1967. RAF 145 Squadron saw action in the Second World War with Hurricane fighters over Dunkirk and in the Battle of Britain, later serving in the Middle East, Malta and Italy.

Merchant Navy Class No. 35003 *Royal Mail* still has a good fire going while waiting on shed at Basingstoke on 1 June 1967. She was built in 1941 and named at Waterloo station by the chairman of the Royal Mail shipping line on 24 October of that year.

Having shunted through the station from the shed, No. 35003 *Royal Mail* waits to haul an evening local from Basingstoke on 1 June 1967. Although she carries a Bournemouth line headcode, my recollection is that the train was actually a local service bound for Salisbury. Notice the vacuum brake-fitted 'Hybar' open wagon on the right.

Preserved A4 Pacific No 4498 *Sir Nigel Gresley*, in LNER Garter Blue livery, catches admiring glances from permanent way staff as she speeds west through Basingstoke hauling an excursion on 5 June 1967. Nigel Gresley's 100th loco, she was built at Doncaster in 1936 and named at Marylebone station by William Whitelaw, chairman of the LNER (who also had an A4 Pacific named after him).

A rather grubby Standard Class 4 2-6-0 No. 76011 waits to pull out from the Down sidings at Basingstoke on 30 June 1967. A 2EPB Electric Multiple Unit is peeping out from behind the signal box.

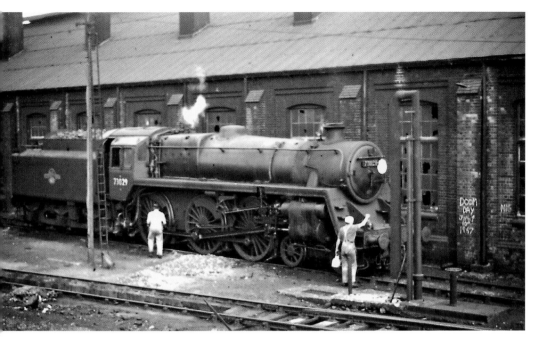

Standard Class 5 No. 73029 was built in 1953. In lined green livery under all the dirt, she is being oiled up ready to depart from Basingstoke shed on 30 June 1967. Note the unique smokebox numberplate carried by this locomotive with its gold coloured characters. A chalked note on the shed wall reminds us that steam's 'Doom Day 9 July 1967' beckons.

In the bay platform at Basingstoke on 30 June 1967 is Battle of Britain Class No. 34089 *602 Squadron*. During the Battle of Britain 602 Squadron flew from West Hampnett, near Chichester, served longest in the front line, and reputedly scored the highest toll of enemy aircraft in the Second World War. Towards the end of the war they attacked the V1 and V2 rocket sites in France. The number of the EPB unit on the left went unrecorded and it appears to be ready to head back towards London.

West Country Class No. 34025 *Whimple* again. This time she immediately precedes the two official Southern Region 'Farewell to Steam' special trains as she approaches Basingstoke on 2 July 1967.

A week before the end of Southern steam, No. 35008 *Orient Line* speeds through Basingstoke heading the first of the official BR 'Farewell to Steam' specials to Weymouth on 2 July 1967. She was named at Waterloo station in November 1942. Notice the contrast in signal boxes behind, with the then new Basingstoke panel box on the left and the old Great Western Railway signal box on the Reading branch.

Hauling the second official 'Farewell to Steam' special train to Bournemouth on 2 July 1967, No. 35028 *Clan Line* cruises west under the Reading Road bridge and through Basingstoke. A family friend from the higher echelons of the Southern Region operating department at Waterloo was riding on the footplate – lucky man!

A relatively clean BR Standard Class 4MT 4-6-0 No. 75074, built at Swindon works in 1955, heads east from Basingstoke on 3 July 1967.

BR Standard Class 5 No. 73029 is on shed at Basingstoke again with a Class 4MT 2-6-0 for company. No doubt they are drawing admiring looks from the enthusiasts on the grass bank between the shed and the Rising Sun public house.

In the shadow of the ruins of the Holy Ghost Chapel across the road, another BR Standard Class 5, believed to be No. 73016, is oiled up in preparation for the road at Basingstoke shed.

In the late afternoon, Merchant Navy 35008 *Orient Line* is leaving Basingstoke at the head of the return Southern Region 'Farewell to Steam' special train from Weymouth to Waterloo.

Not my best, but still a very special picture of No. 35030 *Elder Dempster Lines*. She was named at Southampton Docks on 5 June 1950 by a director of the shipping line. The loco has just a whisp of steam from her safety valves as she rushes the final scheduled Southern Region steam service, the 2.07 p.m. from Weymouth through Basingstoke towards Waterloo on 9 July 1967. The following day, 10 July 1967, full electric services began.

Non-BR Locomotives Keep the Flag Flying for Steam Traction

Ex-London South Western and Southern Railway Class B4 0-4-0T No. 30096, owned by Corralls the coal merchants, shunts at Dibles Wharf on the River Itchen, Southampton, on 2 January 1968. A collier can be seen in the dock.

A head-on portrait. Originally named *Normandy* in Southern Railway days, No. 30096 carried the name *Corrall Queen* while in the ownership of Corralls. She was designed by Adams and built in 1893 at Nine Elms Works, London. A number of now classic lorries can also be seen.

At Dibles Wharf in 1968 *Corrall Queen* shunts some rusty 16-ton coal wagons. She went on to enjoy a new lease of life at the Bluebell Railway where she is still based.

Here No. 30096 is seen shunting 21-ton coal hopper wagons, again at Dibles Wharf for Corralls.

Amid piles of sleepers, ex-GWR London Transport Pannier Tank No. L97 (formerly No. 7749) shunts at Lillie Bridge permanent way depot, near Earls Court Exhibition Centre, on 4 January 1968. Between 1937 and 1946 London Underground engineers pioneered the use of flash welding of long welded rails (now known as Continuous Welded Rail) at Lillie Bridge depot. The area has since been redeveloped.

Catching the afternoon sun as she stands outside the steam shed at Neasden depot on 24 January 1968 is No. L99 (previously WR No. 7715). She was built in 1930 by Kerr, Stuart & Co. Following rebuilding of the depot to handle new trains the shed has since been decommissioned and become the depot's training facility.

Pannier Tank No. L93, the former WR No. 7779, built in 1930 by Armstrong Whitworth & Co, looks as though she may have nearly drawn her last breath as she stands at Neasden depot on 24 January 1968.

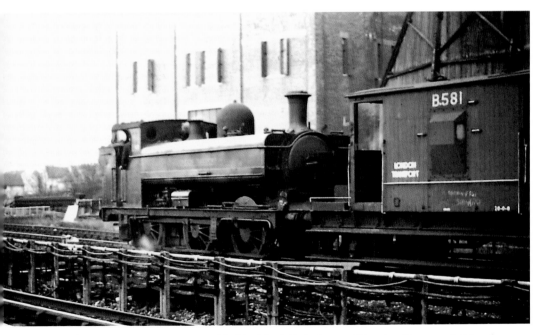

A train of engineer's wagons is assembled by No. L98 in front of London Transport's Neasden power station on 24 January 1968. The power station, the old wooden cooling tower for which is on the right, was opened in 1904 for the Metropolitan Railway and ceased generating in 1968.

The crew exchange words with depot staff before No. L98 sets off from Neasden. No. L98 was built as GWR No. 7739 by the North British Locomotive Company in 1930.

Preparations complete, No. L98 heads away 'down the hole' towards Watford and Croxley Tip. The tip was used for dumping spent ballast, power station waste and loco ash.

Another view of No. L97, this time at Neasden on 24 January 1968, resting between duties. She was built as GWR No. 7749, also by the North British Locomotive Company.

London Transport's 'The Last Drop' on Sunday 6 June 1971 at Neasden. No. L90 (previously WR No. 7760), surrounded by a crowd of about a thousand people, brings to an end steam on London Underground. The loco had earlier hauled an official final steam working from Moorgate station to Neasden depot before dropping her fire for the last time.

Another view of L90 on the occasion of London Transport's 'The Last Drop', showing the crowds that were present at Neasden depot to witness the event.

The British Aluminium Company's works was situated beside the Aberdeen to Edinburgh line at Burntisland, Fife. Here, from a fast-moving train between Aberdeen and Edinburgh in 1970, is glimpsed their No. 1, Peckett 0-4-0T No. 1376 built in 1915, shunting an ICI Mond Division chemical tanker.

Graveyards of Steam

After dropping their fires for the last time on 9 July 1967 the remaining Southern Region steam locos were assembled at Salisbury and Weymouth depots prior to formal disposal and onward transportation to scrapyards in South Wales and elsewhere. The next few pictures illustrate these 'graveyards' and show several locomotives that I was unable to photograph when they were in service.

The loco shown above at Salisbury is Battle of Britain Class No. 34057 *Biggin Hill*, named after the famous Second World War fighter station from where flying aces such as Douglas Bader flew. I always had a soft spot for No. 34057 as it was the prototype for a Kitmaster and later Airfix 00 gauge plastic kit, and I still have my father's superbly made model.

A general view of Salisbury shed on 26 July 1967 showing a variety of Southern Region steam locos. In nautical terms the bridge to engine room telegraph would have shown 'finished with engines'.

USA tank loco No. 30064 was built in 1943 at the Vulcan Ironworks in the USA for the US Army Transportation Corps. After the Second World War several of these USA tanks were bought by the Southern Railway for shunting in Southampton Docks. No. 30064 ended its days as works shunter at Eastleigh. She was rescued before scrapping and is currently located at the Bluebell Railway.

Standard Class 3 2-6-2T No. 82029 was built at Swindon works in 1954. She spent her last few years in service at Nine Elms depot, London, and could be seen hauling empty coaching stock between Waterloo station and Clapham Junction carriage sidings.

Now cold and never expected to draw a fire again, No. 34006 *Bude*, No. 30064, No. 30072, No. 82029 and two Class 4MTs form a melancholy line-up awaiting their final journeys at Salisbury on 26 July 1967. The third loco, No. 30072, was subsequently rescued and can be seen at the Keighley & Worth Valley Railway.

West Country Class No. 34006 *Bude*, which put up such wonderful performances during the 1948 Locomotive Exchanges. She carried the extended length smoke deflectors right until the end. This low angle shot shows the trough around the chimney designed at assist exhaust smoke dispersal.

Battle of Britain Class No. 34088 *213 Squadron* at Basingstoke on 26 July 1967. She has seen better days and carries a wreath on the smokebox door. In 1940 213 Squadron reinforced the British Expeditionary Force and later took part in operations over Dunkirk. From 1941 the squadron flew over the Western Desert in support of the 8th Army and in the last weeks of the Second World War the squadron served in Yugoslavia.

Class 4MT 2-6-4T No. 80134 at rest in the rather shadowy back yard of Weymouth shed on 30 September 1967.

A contrast to 26 May when Ivatt Class 2 tank locomotive No. 41320 enthusiastically banked the Channel Islands Boat train up Parkstone Bank! This dismal view was taken on 30 September 1967 at Weymouth.

Standard Class 3 2-6-0 No. 77014 was previously a North Eastern and London Midland Region loco. She came south to participate in the Locomotive Club of Great Britain 'South Western Suburban Railtour'. She liked it so much on the Southern that she stayed to the end. One of a small class of only twenty locos built at Swindon in 1954, she is seen here, captured with a time exposure, inside Weymouth shed on 30 September 1967.

Slumbering away her last days and bearing inscriptions relating to previous Ocean Liner Boat Train duties is Standard Class 5 No. 73092. She was built at Derby works in 1955 and is seen here in Weymouth shed yard on 30 September 1967.

A final sad view of Weymouth shed yard late in the afternoon of 30 September 1967. The new order is present in the shape of an Esso fuel oil storage tanker, a Crompton diesel locomotive and an 0-6-0 diesel shunter. The old order in the shape of several dead steam locos is also visible.

On 16 March 1968 I visited Woodham's scrapyard at Barry, South Wales. This was early days at Barry and the locomotives were not in the awful state they would be in later decades. Despite their sojourn in the sea air they still bore their liveries, if a little faded. On a happier note, all the locos here have since been saved, even if they are not yet all restored or in service.

This view shows ex-Somerset & Dorset Joint Railway Fowler Class 7F 2-8-0 No. 53808. She was built in 1925 and withdrawn in 1964, when she ended up at Barry scrapyard. After restoration she spent some years painted S&DJR blue livery on the West Somerset Railway and is due to move to the Watercress Line.

LMS Jinty 0-6-0T No. 47357, Black 5 No. 45491, Merchant Navy No. 35005 *Canadian Pacific*, and Ivatt 2-6-2T No. 41312 are lined up in the sunshine, unknowingly waiting better days.

The solitary British Railways Standard Class 8, No. 71000 *Duke of Gloucester*. What a sad sight. She was designed at Derby and built at Crewe in 1953. Instead of the whole loco, just one cylinder and set of Caprotti rotary cam poppet valve gear went to the Science Museum, London. The left cylinder and valve gear was used as a guinea pig for the sectioning of the right one. Remarkably, after considerable remanufacturing this loco now roams the main line again.

Modified Hall No. 7927 *Willington Hall* was built by BR in 1950. Her frames have gone to the 1014 *County of Glamorgan* Project (with the boiler of 8F 48518) and her boiler to the *Betton Grange* 6880 project, to recreate examples of County and Grange class locos, none of which survived.

Ivatt Class 2 2-6-0 No. 46428, built at Crewe in 1948, basks in the sun. No. 46428 is now at the East Lancs Railway undergoing restoration.

Battle of Britain Class No. 34059 *Sir Archibald Sinclair* was built in Brighton in 1947. Sinclair served as Minister for Air in Winston Churchill's wartime coalition government. He worked with the Royal Air Force in planning the Battle of Britain and later in the war argued against the bombing of Dresden. The loco is currently undergoing overhaul on the Bluebell Railway.

West Country Class No. 34105 *Swanage* was built in 1950 at Brighton. In 1951 she hauled the inaugural 'Royal Wessex' express from Weymouth to Waterloo. As well as the main line she also worked on the Somerset & Dorset Joint route and is currently based at the Watercress Line in Hampshire.

Stanier Jubilee Class No. 45690 *Leander* was built at Crewe in 1936. She was named after the Royal Navy ship and the Greek hero of that name and currently resides at Carnforth.

GWR King Class loco No. 6024 *King Edward I* was built in 1930 and withdrawn in June 1962 after completing over 1.5 million miles in traffic. Initially she went to the Buckinghamshire Railway Centre at Quainton Road for restoration before running for many years on the main line. The loco is currently undergoing heavy repairs.

Battle of Britain Class No. 34070 *Manston* was the last loco to be numbered with the system used by Bulleid, emerging from Brighton works in 1947 as No. 21C170. Located on the Isle of Thanet, Manston aerodrome was equipped initially with Hawker Hurricane fighters. The loco is currently under repair at the Swanage Railway. To the left is a pair of Pannier Tanks and on the right is the cab of a Great Western Small Prairie with sloping-top side tanks.

West Country Class No. 34092 *City of Wells* and an unidentified LMS Jinty 0-6-0T. No. 34092 was built at Brighton in 1949 and initially named *Wells*, this being changed to *City of Wells* in 1950. In more recent years following restoration, this loco has excelled itself out on the main line and is now based on the East Lancs Railway.

The S15 class was initially designed by Urie and later improved by Maunsell. No. 30825 was built in 1927 at Eastleigh works. In preservation No. 30825 has swapped parts with No. 30841, which experienced brief fame as the *Greene King* loco, named after a brewery, and is currently based at the North Yorkshire Moors Railway.

Although the 8F 2-8-0s were a Stanier LMS design of 1935, some were built elsewhere during the LMS era and the war years. No. 48431 was constructed at Swindon works in 1944 under the auspices of the wartime Railway Executive Committee. She was withdrawn from Bath Green Park shed in May 1964 and sent from there to Barry. The nineteenth loco rescued from Barry, she was transported to the Keighley & Worth Valley Railway and re-entered service there in late 1975.

A view from the cab of No. 5080 *Defiant* of a row of ex-GW tank engines. *Defiant* was originally built as *Ogmore Castle* in 1939 and renamed after the fighter aircraft in 1941. *Defiant* is now part of the Vintage Trains excursion fleet at Tyseley depot and is undergoing overhaul to main line standards.

Collett Big Prairie No. 4141 is seen here at Barry with the old Lion on Wheel BR crest. After entering service from Swindon works in 1946 she spent her whole working life at Gloucester. In preservation she has appeared at the Severn Valley, Llangollen and Great Central railways and is now at the Epping & Ongar railway.

Hawksworth Pannier Tank No. 9406 was one of a batch of only ten such locos built by the GWR. After nationalisation a further 200 were constructed by various builders. Nos 9406 and 9400 are both preserved, with the latter forming part of the national collection.

Riddles BR Standard Class 9F 2-10-0 No. 92207 was built at Swindon in 1959, the thirteenth from last. She is numerically close to both No. 92203 *Black Prince* and No. 92220 *Evening Star*. She was one of the 9F locos fitted with a double chimney and is still undergoing restoration.

GWR Hall Class loco No. 4983 *Albert Hall*, prototype of the well-known Triang-Hornby model, or so it seemed to me back in 1968. During restoration, which took thirty-one years, it transpired that this loco contains parts from No. 4965 *Rood Ashton Hall*. She now carries name and numberplates from both locos but is usually attached to *Rood Ashton Hall*'s 3,500-gallon tender, rather than the Hawksworth flat-sided tender with which she is partnered here. On the left is the tender of Castle Class *Defiant* and on the right the front of Jubilee *Leander*.

This picture shows GWR 0-6-2T No. 5637 and the front of SR N Class 2-6-0 No. 31874. No. 5637 was built at Swindon in 1925 and spent its life in South Wales. The class was designed to replace indigenous locos of the various South Wales companies and usually ran up the valleys smokebox-first and back down bunker-first with the pony truck giving greater stability on the descent. No. 5637 is currently at the East Somerset Railway.

GWR 2-6-0 No. 5322 was built during the First World War in 1917 and sent for service in France, from where she returned in 1919. On withdrawal No. 5322 was the sole loco of this type without a side window cab at Barry. This venerable loco was the first GWR loco to leave Barry, being preserved by the Great Western Society Caerphilly Group in 1969, and now based at Didcot. Behind her is 2-8-0T No. 4247, built in 1916 and which spent most of its life in South Wales. Withdrawn in 1964 and rescued in 1985, No. 4247 has spent time at several heritage lines and is now on the Bodmin & Wenford Railway.

GWR 0-6-2T No. 6686 is appropriately inscribed 'Thus an era ends'. Built by Armstrong Whitworth in 1928, she spent almost her entire life in South Wales. One of the last 'Barry Ten' locos bought by Vale of Glamorgan Council just before Dai Woodhams retired. This loco is, perhaps appropriately, under restoration for eventual use on the Barry Tourist Railway.

Early Preservation Years

In pouring rain, *Merddin Emrys* and *Prince* double head a train into Portmadoc Harbour station on the Ffestiniog Railway in 1968.

Built at the Boston Lodge Works of the Ffestiniog Railway in 1879, Double Fairlie loco *Merddin Emrys* is seen shunting from the Cob into Boston Lodge, site of the shed and works.

Originally built in 1883 for service in Penrhyn Quarry, *Linda* is a 2-4-0 Saddle Tank and Tender loco. She came to the Ffestiniog Railway in 1962 and is seen here receiving a top-up of water after arriving at Tan-y-Bwlch.

One of the Ffestiniog Railway's original locomotives, *Prince* was built in 1863. Here *Prince* takes a breather after arriving at Tan-y-Bwlch in 1968. Shortly after this picture was taken the loco was withdrawn for rebuilding.

Named after the mountain it spends its life climbing, Snowdon Mountain Railway rack loco No. 4 *Snowdon* makes ready to head away from Llanberis. The 0-4-2T loco was built in 1896 by the Swiss Locomotive & Machine Works at Winterthur, Switzerland, and in this picture was over seventy years old.

Polished up to within an inch of her life, No. 4079 *Pendennis Castle* proudly carries the prestigious 'Bristolian' headboard at a Great Western Society Reading Group open day at Taplow goods yard. The souvenir car parking ticket confirms the date as Saturday 16 September 1967.

Where are the crowds that would be seen today, and I wonder where these folk are now? There is only a rope to separate the visitors from the BR high-speed main line tracks. No. 4079 *Pendennis Castle* at the Taplow open day again; I hadn't learnt to be patient enough to wait until the view was clear!

Collett 'baby castle' 0-6-0 No. 3205, built by the GWR in 1946, shuttles up and down at Taplow. She hauled the first passenger train when the Severn Valley Railway reopened in 1970 and is now located on the South Devon Railway. The wagon in the background with three vertical white stripes painted on the side is a shock-absorbing wagon with longitudinal springs separating the body and chassis, designed to carry delicate loads such as crates of plate glass.

Privately owned Big Prairie 2-6-2T No. 6106 gives rides in the Great Western Railway Super Saloons, No. 9112 *Queen Mary* and No. 9113 *Prince of Wales* at Taplow on 16 September 1967. Note how wide the ex-Great Western Railway Super Saloons were, benefitting from broad gauge clearances. They were the equivalent of Pullman Cars and are now based at the Great Western Society's Didcot depot together with Super Saloon kitchen car 9118 *Princess Elizabeth*.

The same loco, No. 6106, is seen again on the same date. Prior to the move to Southampton as the terminal for ocean liners, the Super Saloons ran in the GWR Ocean Liner Boat Expresses between Plymouth and Paddington, saving vital time for those well-heeled passengers who wished to reach the capital in a hurry.

Another picture of a very resplendent No. 4079 *Pendennis Castle*. The wheel hubs are lined out in orange and the mainframes are painted red. Whether they ever were during No. 4079's service life I don't know. The connecting and coupling rods shine almost as if they are silver plated!

Receiving attention at the Dowty preservation centre at Ashchurch during the early stages of their preservation are No. 7808 *Cookham Manor* and 0-6-2T No. 6697. No. 7808 was the only Manor to be bought directly out of service from BR. These two locos were transferred to the Great Western Society site at Didcot in 1970. Due to the GWR's urgent need for such locos No. 6697 was built by Armstrong Whitworth of Newcastle.

Maunsell Schools Class No. 928 *Stowe* stands as a static exhibit at what was then the Beaulieu Motor Museum, now the National Motor Museum. She was initially preserved by Lord Montague of Beaulieu, her connecting rods and valve gear receiving a protective coating. The Schools class locos were the most powerful 4-4-0s in Britain. *Stowe* is now at the Bluebell Railway, along with one of the Pullman Cars shown here, *Fingal*.

Taking water at the Longmoor Military Railway in 1968 is 34023 *Blackmore Vale*. She was bought directly out of BR service by a group of drivers and their colleagues from Nine Elms depot who formed the Bulleid Pacific Preservation Society. She was fitted with a Southern Railway ownership disc on the smokebox door, which shows the date the loco was built, 1946. Alternative spellings for the name are *Blackmoor Vale* (Southern Railway malachite green livery days) and *Blackmore Vale* (British Railways days). She has also at times carried an *OVS Bulleid* nameplate to commemorate her designer.

BR Standard Class 9F 2-10-0 No. 92203 was preserved straight out of BR service in 1967 by the renowned wildlife artist David Shepherd. She is shown here arriving at Longmoor Downs station on the Longmoor Military Railway with the 'Bulleid Commemorative Rail Tour'.

Following arrival at Longmoor on the above-mentioned rail tour on 8 June 1968, No. 92203 traverses the level crossing en route to the depot at Longmoor. Prior to her naming ceremony, the nameplates are (nearly) covered by a curtain! The 'Bulleid Commemorative Rail Tour' ran from Waterloo via Clapham Junction, Haywards Heath, Lewes, Brighton, Havant and Liss.

Having never carried a name in her BR days, David Shepherd brightened up No. 92203 by lining out the loco and tender in orange. At this Longmoor open day on 8 June 1968 Major General E. H. G. Lonsdale is naming her *Black Prince*. David Shepherd, in the drivers' greasetop cap, had to manually push the curtain back to reveal the Swindon-made *Black Prince* nameplate.

Merchant Navy Class No. 35028 *Clan Line* was built in 1948 at Eastleigh, named by Lord Rotherwick, chairman of the shipping line and rebuilt in 1959. Following purchase direct from BR service in August 1967 by the Merchant Navy Locomotive Preservation Society, she was initially based at Longmoor where she is seen here. She is now a regular performer on the main line, often at the head of the former 'Venice Simplon Orient Express', now 'Belmond' British Pullman train.

War Department 0-6-0T No. 196 was built in 1953 by the Hunslet Engine Company to the War Department Austerity design and spent its working life on the Longmoor Military Railway. She was named *Errol Lonsdale* on 8 January 1968. After spending time at the Mid-Hants and South Devon railways, *Errol Lonsdale* is now at the Stoomcentrum Maldegem, a museum in Belgium.

Another picture of No. 34023 *Blackmore Vale* looking very spick and span at a Longmoor open day. With the closure of the Longmoor Military Railway, No. 34023 was moved by rail to Haywards Heath and then by road to the Bluebell Railway where she still is. She entered service on the Bluebell Railway in 1976 after a thorough overhaul and return to Southern Railway condition with shortened smoke deflectors, built up sides to the tender and malachite green livery with three yellow stripes.

Built at Swindon in 1936, and originally numbered 4866, this 0-4-2 tank loco was renumbered 1466 in the 1940s. She was the first loco bought by the Great Western Society in 1964 and was initially based at their Totnes depot. She is seen here on a Great Western Society running day after arrival at Cholsey station.

Under a rather threatening sky, No. 1466 is seen here at Wallingford on the same Great Western Society running day with auto coach 231. The two GWR Super Saloons can be seen in the background. Sixty years after her preservation was first mooted she is under overhaul, and it is hoped to have No. 1466 back in working order in 2021.

Preserved GWR Prairie Tank No. 6106 features in this picture with Fowler Showman's Road Locomotive *Renown* taken at the Great Western Society Wallingford running day. Now owned by the Howard Brothers of Derbyshire, *Renown* was originally built in 1920 for showman John Murphy to travel his 'Proud Peacocks' scenic railway ride.

At the last Longmoor open day on 5 July 1969, War Department Austerity 2-10-0 No. 600 *Gordon* arrives at Longmoor Downs with a three-coach train of aged ex-Southern Railway stock. She was built in 1943 by the North British Locomotive Company at their Glasgow Hyde Park works and looks magnificent in the Longmoor Military Railway blue and red livery.

A really impressive loco at close quarters! No. 600 *Gordon* approaches and crosses the road as she nears Longmoor Downs station. Although built for overseas service, *Gordon* served as a training loco at Longmoor with the Royal Engineers. This mighty locomotive is now resident on the Severn Valley Railway and takes pride of place in The Engine House at Highley.

Here we have another view of No. 600 *Gordon* crossing the road en route to Longmoor Downs station.

Ivatt 2-6-2T No. 41298 is seen at Longmoor in 1969. She was built in the year of my birth, 1951, at the famous Crewe works. She spent her life on the Southern Region in Devon and the London area and was bought straight out of BR service in 1967 by the Ivatt Locomotive Society. She is now in the ownership of and resident at the Isle of Wight Steam Railway.

A view of Longmoor Downs yard with three locos visible: Merchant Navy No. 35028 *Clan Line* on the left, WD No. 600 *Gordon* at centre and the then relatively new Sentinel 0-8-0 diesel WD No. 890 *General Lord Robertson* on the embankment.

A view of Class 4MT 4-6-0 No. 75029 *The Green Knight* at the July 1969 Longmoor Military Railway open day sporting the headboard of the famed 'Cambrian Coast Express'. She was also built in 1951, fitted with a double chimney in 1957 and was basically a tender version of the BR Standard 2-6-4 tank.

A broadside view of No. 75029 *The Green Knight* on the same occasion. After going to David Shepherd's preservation site at Cranmore following the closure of Longmoor, she is now based on the North Yorkshire Moors Railway and is also passed to run between Grosmont and Whitby.

WD No. 600 *Gordon* crosses the girder bridge over the approach to Longmoor depot yard.

On 5 July 1969, No. 75029's name *The Green Knight* is unveiled by her owner, David Shepherd. She served mainly on the Western Region and following withdrawal in 1967 was bought directly from BR. The name had previously been carried by Southern Railway King Arthur Class No. 754 and was later transferred to BR Standard Class 5 No. 73086 before adorning No. 75029.

David Shepherd toasts the future of No. 75029 *The Green Knight* at Longmoor on 5 July 1969. The idea of a steam preservation centre at Longmoor gave hope of a permanent home for the owners of the various locomotives based there in the mid-1960s. At the time, the Longmoor Military Railway was a self-contained network of lines connected to the BR Waterloo–Portsmouth main line at Liss and had its own workshop facilities. However, objections to planning applications were made by local residents, who also bought sections of the site to prevent reuse, and the proposal fell. David set up his own railway preservation centre in 1972 at Cranmore, later to be known as the East Somerset Railway, and the other locos were dispersed to various preserved lines and depots.

Also seen at Longmoor is 0-4-0ST *Lord Fisher*, built by Andrew Barclay in 1915. While initially in use at the Royal Naval Airship Station at Rochester, Kent, she was named after the British admiral and is here being renamed by Major General Errol Lonsdale. *Lord Fisher* can now be seen at the Yeovil Railway Centre.

The loco *Lord Fisher* has also seen use at the Royal Aircraft Establishment in Farnborough and several other locations, and was purchased for preservation in 1967. Notice the wooden dumb buffers carried by this loco and the line of (empty!) ale bottles on the footplate following her renaming.

A change of scene sees us in the South Devon countryside at Buckfastleigh where GWR 2-6-2 Small Prairie tank locomotive No. 4555 approaches Buckfastleigh station on the Dart Valley Railway, now known as the South Devon Railway.

Here we see the level crossing at Staverton Bridge station. When the line was closed by BR this GWR crossing keeper's hut was bought by a local vicar to serve as a potting shed, but reopening of the line saw the hut returned to its original site and purpose.

GWR 2-6-2T No. 4555, built in 1924 and bought straight out of service from BR in 1965, attracts attention on arrival at Buckfastleigh station. During the last years of BR operation this loco had been used to haul goods trains on the Ashburton branch.

Looking rather well used in Buckfastleigh station yard we see 0-4-2T No. 1420. She was built at Swindon in 1933 as No. 4820, spent most of her life in and around Wales, and arrived at Buckfastleigh in 1965. Beyond her is very pristine 0-6-0 Pannier Tank No. 1369. Fitted with outside cylinders, she was designed in 1910 to replace some older dock shunting locos and was used on Weymouth Quay for shunting and hauling boat trains along the tramway to Weymouth station.

This view of No. 4555 running round her train at Buckfastleigh is not now possible. The presence of the embankment for the A38 South Devon Expressway dual carriageway road and various rolling stock sheds on the right now foreshorten the view.

No. 1420 looks much more resplendent in this picture taken at Ashburton station. The goods shed is on the right and the branch tracks had not yet been severed by the A38 dual carriageway.

Not strictly a GWR engine as she was built after nationalisation by BR in 1951. No. 1638 is a powerful 0-6-0 Pannier Tank and carries the short-lived 'Dart Valley' branding on her tank sides. Photographed here under the lovely overall roof at Ashburton station, No. 1638 now resides on the Kent & East Sussex Railway.

A GWR idyll! Ashburton station on a lovely summer day is host to locos Nos 1420 and 1638. The broad gauge clearances to both goods shed and station are evident in this view. The Dart Valley Railway briefly reopened as far as Ashburton in 1969 but prior to the A38 road improvements the station finally closed in 1971 and its future is uncertain.

One of the Dart Valley Railway's Pannier Tanks undergoes an overhaul at Ashburton and receives close inspection by my parents and my brother, Roger. The loco is supported on jacks and the removal of the bufferbeam has allowed the inside cylinders to be exposed.

Early days at the Great Western Society's Didcot Railway Centre sees a line-up of GWR and other locos on 19 September 1970. Wantage Tramway Well Tank loco No. 5, 0-4-2T No. 1466, 0-6-2T No. 6697 and streamlined 'Flying Banana' railcar 4 are on view.

Seen here at Didcot Railway Centre, 0-4-0ST *Bonnie Prince Charlie* was built by Robert Stephenson & Hawthorns in 1949 for Corralls Ltd and initially worked at Hamworthy Wharf, Poole. The loco was moved by Corralls to Dibles Wharf, Southampton, in 1965 and purchased for preservation in 1969 by the Salisbury Steam Trust. When I saw B4 tank No. 30096 at Corralls' Dibles Wharf in 1968 this loco appeared to be derelict at the end of the wharf.

Big Prairie No. 6106 goes from strength to strength, seen here giving rides at Didcot Railway Centre on 19 September 1970.

Bagnall fireless locomotive No. 2473 was purchased by Huntley & Palmers, biscuit manufacturers of Reading, in 1932 to shunt wagons within the factory. Seen here at Didcot, she moved to the Cholsey & Wallingford Railway, and is now in Yorkshire. One charge of steam to 220 psi gave her a two-hour range of action.

Castle Class No. 5051 was built in 1936. She was withdrawn and sent to Woodham's scrapyard, Barry, in 1963, being rescued in 1970 when this photograph was taken at Didcot. Originally named *Drysllwyn Castle*, she was later renamed *Earl Bathhurst* and both names have been used in preservation.

By contrast is No. 4079 *Pendennis Castle*, again seen at Didcot on 19 September 1970 in the ownership of the Hon. John Gretton and Sir William McAlpine. In 1977 she was sold to the Hammersley Iron Railway, Australia, but was returned to the Great Western Society at Didcot in 2000. She was one of four locos selected by the Western Region to haul 'Farewell to Steam' runs from Paddington to Plymouth in 1964 when she attained 96 mph.

The Southern Electric Group's 'Man of Kent' Railtour on 11 April 1971 included a visit to the Ashford Steam Centre, where South Eastern Railway O1 Class loco No. 65 is seen in the company of two Pullman Cars. These engines were designed by Stirling in 1906 and rebuilt to this form in 1908. The above-frame tender springs give a truly vintage feel to the loco. Following preservation in 1963 she is now doing sterling work on the Bluebell Railway.

South Eastern H Class tank loco No. 263 is also seen here at Ashford Steam Centre in April 1971, in the company of a 'birdcage' brake coach. These engines were to be seen on many country branch lines in Sussex and this loco is known to have worked on the former line between East Grinstead and Three Bridges. She was constructed in 1905, withdrawn as No. 31263 in 1964 and moved to the Bluebell Railway in 1976. The Ashford site has since been sold for housing development.

The 'Man of Kent' tour also took in the Sittingbourne & Kemsley Light Railway, where we see 0-6-2 tank loco *Triumph*. The railway was constructed in 1905 to serve Bowaters Paper Mill, to bring in raw materials and move around the finished products. *Triumph* was built by W. G. Bagnall in 1934.

Also on 11 April 1971, 2 foot 6 inch gauge *Triumph* wends her way through the Bowater industrial installations, all of which looks rather different now. In 2020 the Sittingbourne & Kemsley Light Railway celebrated fifty years as a public railway.

The 'Man of Kent' tour also included a visit to the Kent & East Sussex Railway, where their Terrier 0-6-0T *Bodiam* is seen, together with the front end of Terrier *Sutton* on the left.

Stanier magnificence is seen in the shape of Princess Coronation or Duchess Pacific No. 6229 *Duchess of Hamilton*. Built in 1938 at Crewe works, she was shipped to America disguised as No. 6220 *Coronation* for exhibition at the 1939 New York World's Fair. By 1947 she had lost her original streamlined casing and was eventually withdrawn by BR in 1964. She was bought by Sir Billy Butlin and exhibited at his Minehead holiday camp where she is pictured here. Acquired by the National Railway Museum in 1976, her streamlined casing was replaced in 2009 by Tyseley Locomotive Works.

Jubilee Class loco No. 5596, named *Bahamas*, was built by the North British Locomotive Co in 1934. She was withdrawn in 1966 and purchased for preservation in 1967. After repair by the Hunslet Engine Co., and reputedly being painted in Humbrol crimson lake modelling enamel, she came to the Dinting Railway Centre, Glossop, where she is seen here on 3 April 1972. Later she moved to the Keighley & Worth Valley Railway and also undertakes main line runs.

Built by Hudswell Clarke of Leeds in 1938 for a firm of cement manufacturers, *Nunlow* is also seen here at Dinting Railway Centre in 1972. After being in store from 1964, she was first steamed at Dinting in 1969 and is painted in a representation of Great Central Railway livery. Along with *Bahamas* she is now at Ingrow on the Keighley & Worth Valley Railway.

Baguley Cars No. 680, also seen here at Dinting, is reputed to be the oldest standard gauge petrol locomotive in the world. No. 680 was delivered new in 1916 to a Manchester firm and later sold to the W. & R. Jacobs Biscuit Factory at Aintree, Liverpool. Until the arrival of a battery loco in 1923 she was their principal locomotive. In due course No. 680 was transferred to the Northern Regional Museum and later the Bowes Museum.

LMS Royal Scot Class No. 6115 *Scots Guardsman* is seen at Dinting while undergoing overhaul. Originally built at the Springburn Works of the North British Locomotive Company in Glasgow, she was rebuilt with a taper boiler in 1947. Preserved in 1969, she now appears on the main line and is based at Carnforth. *Scots Guardsman* was one of five locomotives that took part in the 2012 Olympic Torch Relay.

GWR Small Prairie No. 4588, one of the later series with larger, sloping-top side tanks, was built at Swindon in 1927. She spent most of her working life in Cornwall, allocated to Truro for many years. After withdrawal in 1962, No. 4588 went to Woodham's Barry scrapyard from where she was rescued by the Dart Valley Railway Association in 1971. Following purchase of the Paignton–Kingswear line she was transferred there. This picture shows her on one of the River Dart bridges near Buckfastleigh.

With small side tanks evident, No. 4555 is seen here, with 'Devon Belle' observation car 13 in tow, as she leaves Buckfastleigh station. The 'Devon Belle' was a relatively short-lived Pullman train between Waterloo and Ilfracombe from 1947 to 1954. This observation car is now on the Torbay & Dartmouth Railway and the other, 14, after returning from the USA in 1969 with *Flying Scotsman* is on the Swanage Railway.

Another view showing No. 4555 departing from Buckfastleigh station bunker first, and waiting for a signal to be pulled off. She is hauling a nice train comprised of the 'Devon Belle' observation car and other GWR carriages.

Here we see No. 4588 again, this time on the Paignton to Kingswear line, now known as the Torbay & Dartmouth Railway. She is ready to leave Kingswear and head into the sun towards Paignton. The first coach is one of the BR-built auto-coaches 228.

A tranquil scene in the days when yachts were free to swing on moorings! The peace is only interrupted by seagulls and the chuff of No. 4588 with three auto-coaches in tow. She is heading away from Kingswear alongside the River Dart, which is somewhat wider here than at Buckfastleigh.

Shown here on a plinth in Tiverton, 0-4-2 tank loco No. 1442 was built at Swindon in 1935. She spent her last years working the 'Tivvy Bumper' local train service between Tiverton and Tiverton Junction stations and was preserved by Lord Amory in 1965. This picture was taken around 1972 en route to a holiday in Cornwall, and in 1978 she was moved inside the Tiverton Museum of Mid Devon Life where she is on static display.

Arriving at Eastleigh depot on the Sunday 13 May 1973 open day is Class 9F 2-10-0 No. 92203 *Black Prince*. Health and safety would now require barriers to prevent onlookers from wandering over the tracks. The open day at the works and depot was held by BR Engineering Ltd and BR Southern Region to raise funds for the Southern Railwaymen's Home for Children at Woking.

As she enters Eastleigh depot No. 92203 *Black Prince* looks rather different compared with her days at Longmoor. The loco has lost her orange lining and gained brass cab-side numerals. The loco crew appear to be keeping a good lookout. On that day *Black Prince* hauled several excursions to Romsey and back via Chandlers Ford.

GWR 0-4-2 tank loco No. 1450 is seen here in charge of 'The Centenarian' train commemorating 100 years of the 'Marlow Donkey' on the Bourne End to Marlow branch line on 15 July 1973. The train consisted of two auto-coaches, one GWR and the other a BR-built Hawksworth design.

In a festive atmosphere with bunting flying, the two auto-coaches making up 'The Centenarian' are seen here at Marlow station with No. 1450 at the buffers.

Steam trains in leafy suburbia! Also seen on 15 July 1973, the Maidenhead to Bourne End steam shuttle trains were topped and tailed by No. 6998 *Burton Agnes Hall* (seen here) and Big Prairie No. 6106.

The Maidenhead to Bourne End shuttle train is seen again with No. 6106 assisting at the rear.

My lineside trainspotting days at this location are remembered in this picture of preserved No. 35028 *Clan Line* as she speeds past the fields at Winklebury between Worting Junction and Basingstoke. Following BR's main line steam ban in the early 1970s, *Clan Line* became one of the small number of locos approved for main line steam excursions. This picture shows the return leg from Westbury to Basingstoke of her first main line special in preservation on 27 April 1974.

The 999th Standard locomotive and last steam loco built by British Railways, Class
9F No. 92220 *Evening Star* is seen here at the Great Western Society's Didcot Steam
Centre. She was completed in 1960 with her typical GWR copper-capped chimney
and painted in BR passenger livery of lined Brunswick green. *Evening Star* was named
in Swindon works and her unique status is commemorated by plaques below each
nameplate. In 1965, after only five years of service, she was withdrawn and put into
preservation, as planned when she was built.

London Brighton & South Coast Railway 0-4-2 No. 214 *Gladstone* is seen here visiting
Sheffield Park on the Bluebell Railway in 1982. The occasion was the celebration of
the centenary of the Lewes & East Grinstead Railway. Designed by William Stroudley,
Gladstone was built at Brighton works in 1882. She was preserved as long ago as 1927
by the Stephenson Locomotive Society, whose president was then J. N. Maskelyne,
railway and model railway author. In 1959 she was donated by them to the British
Transport Commission on condition that she was repainted in original livery.

A brace of BR Standard Class 4s, Nos 80064 and 75027, is seen in tandem at Horsted Keynes on the Bluebell Railway. The latter engine is currently on display at Sheffield Park pending overhaul and return to service.

At Sheffield Park P Class No. 323 *Bluebell* and Terrier Tank No. 55 *Stepney* are seen double heading. *Bluebell* was built in 1910 and arrived at the Bluebell Railway in 1960. She last worked in 2019. *Stepney* was built in 1875 and is shown in Stroudley's Golden Ochre livery.

Echoes of the 'Atlantic Coast Express' as pristine Bulleid Pacific No. 34023 *Blackmore Vale*, in 1950s condition and with a nice train of Bulleid carriages in tow, is ready to depart from the Bluebell Railway's Sheffield Park station. She currently awaits overhaul, which will include a new firebox. Notice how the profiles of the cab and tender match that of the Bulleid carriages.

Moments later North London Railway 0-6-0T No. 58850 (or LMS No. 27505), double heading with another locomotive, enters Sheffield Park station. However, she is pointing the wrong way to go to Broad Street. She arrived on the Bluebell Railway in 1962 and when her turn for overhaul comes around she too will need a new firebox.

Maunsell Q Class 0-6-0 No. 541, in Southern Railway black livery, enters Horsted Keynes station. She was built in the first year of the Second World War, 1939, and arrived at the Bluebell Railway in 1978. She is regarded as a good workhorse and has recently visited several other heritage lines.

A view of an interloper from the Great Western Railway in the form of Dukedog class 4-4-0 No. 9017 *Earl of Berkeley*. She is ready to leave the Bluebell Railway's Sheffield Park station with a train of Southern Railway high-capacity compartment coaches.

Highly polished Maunsell Q Class 0-6-0 No. 541 is a credit to the Maunsell Locomotive Society and the Bluebell Railway locomotive department. She is seen again as the driver enjoys chatting to a member of the public prior to departure from Sheffield Park station.

Resplendent in Southern Railway livery, Schools Class 4-4-0 *Stowe* is ready to head north from Sheffield Park towards Horsted Keynes. Behind her is one of several of the Bluebell Railway's magnificently restored Maunsell carriages, a corridor brake composite. A fitting Maunsell train for a superb Maunsell locomotive.

No. 323 *Bluebell* waits at Horsted Keynes with a demonstration goods train. In the adjacent line is the London North Western Railway observation saloon 1503, built in 1913 and painted in the livery of that company.

Magnificently renovated No. 34016 *Bodmin* makes a smoky start from Alresford station on the Watercress Line in Hampshire. She was built in 1945 and allocated to Exmouth Junction shed. Following rebuilding in 1958 she moved to Ramsgate. Her final years were spent at Eastleigh until withdrawal in 1964 and transfer to Woodham's scrapyard at Barry, from where she was rescued in 1972.

Memories of the 'Bournemouth Belle' as No. 34016 *Bodmin* leaves Ropley station. Ropley is the site of the Watercress or Mid-Hants Line locomotive facilities. I remember that when *Bodmin* re-entered service in 1979 following 30,000 hours of restoration, she was a glorious sight to behold and was rightly commended in the annual Association of Railway Preservation Societies' awards.

LSWR T9 Class 4-4-0 No. 30120 was built in 1899 at Nine Elms. In 1962, having been withdrawn the year before, she was repainted by BR into LSWR colours and put back into service working special trains. Here she awaits departure from Alresford on the Watercress Line. She is one of the National locomotive collection and has visited various heritage lines in recent years.

To end we see the sheer might of a Merchant Navy Class locomotive as No. 35027 *Port Line* awaits departure from Sheffield Park on the Bluebell Railway. *Port Line* was built in 1948 and initially allocated to Bournemouth. She was withdrawn in 1966 and sent to Woodham's scrapyard, Barry. From there she was rescued in 1982 and became the first Merchant Navy from Barry to be returned to steam.